I0172458

I Swallowed The Wrong Sky !

Adithya C S

BookLeaf
Publishing

India | USA | UK

Made with ❤ on the BookLeaf Publishing Platform
www.bookleafpub.in
www.bookleafpub.com

Dedication

"For the child I once was, the person I've become; for everyone I've lost, for the love of my parents—and for you, you know why."

Preface

If you expect a hug of comfort , a pat on the shoulder or
even a look of sympathy for everything you've
experienced , This collection is intend to make you feel
uncomfortable. For every individual who have been
through a roller coaster of emotions between the blink of
an eye , who spend their nights being scared of the people
outside, feeling helpless and unheard, mourning the lose
of a loved one or the ones who perceive life from a
different perspective. Each and every word here weighs a
tone from grief , guilt, love and every strange emotions of
human experience. Each poem is supposed to make you
feel how weirdly unsettling our life is and how important
it is to notice the haunting beauty in everything we ignore.

I started writing when I was only ten years old. A journal,
a poem , a story , just anything and everything that came
to my mind , was splattered across the torn page of my old
notebooks. I criticised my work to a point I thought they
would never see the light of the day. But a moment of
impulsiveness is the sole reason for the existence of this
book.

I intend this collection to be a reminder of the dark face of life , the beauty ,the agony and the irony of things .The way life purposefully creates chaos in the midst of a random day; The way we fall for falsity and everything influencing us with mere hope of attention.I hope every poem raises a question in you, that if life and death are twin shadows cast by the same dying sun or is it quite the opposite.

To all whom this little book may come to , I hope you heal from the indignity of loss you endured. I wish your existence make sense to yourself and that someday you'll be kind enough to embrace the feelings that seemed unworthy of your love.

This collection is not a sanctuary, but a threshold. An act of freedom from a self built cage. I will consider myself a successful poet , if I could help you make sense of a feeling you never wanted to feel; For life is all about our journey and not the destination, I would consider myself a lucky one. To quote Gillian flynn " Dark sides are important. They should be nurtured like nasty black orchids"

Acknowledgements

" *With deepest appreciation to my quiet anchor, who knows these pages as well as I do, for their guidance and support ; to Bookleaf publishing for bringing my dream into a reality and to the Universe for granting me the inspiration and strength to see this work come to life.*"

1. Under the magnolia tree

How painful it is to lay on my bed
as darkness creeps through my skull
longing for nothing
knowing noone is looking for my face in a crowd .
How isolating it is to lay here by myself in agony
there's nowhere I would rather be
This self made prison of mine
that I've been chained and tormented .

How pathetic of me to yearn for a touch ,
a whisper in my ears,
to be heard and to be yearned ,
longed to touch my skin
my blood , my smell, my tears .
How could I even exist ,
without a tiny soul wrapped around me
Like a coat , an umbrella in a storm .

My thoughts sank my heart in agony
creating pain and brutal nightmares ,
eating my insides like a parasite ,

every bit of my light , my joy ,
everything I held dear of .

The slow breath and an aimless gaze
Into the ceiling fan, a closed wooden door .
A room full of lies and monsters hiding under my bed ,
a beating heart, that's all there is
half alive half demise .

My body is frigid and so is my heart ;
my hands are away from everything warm ,
leaving what I once loved ,
leaving myself into an abyss of woe.
Did I ruin myself ? or was it someone else ?
Was this deserved or is this my end ?
Am I finally paying for my sins ?
Is this my unexpected fate?
For as I deserve no kindness .

Rest my head on my lover's lap
let me know what warmth feels like .
Mend my heart with your love ,
let me kiss your face , your eyes ;
Those beautiful brown eyes .

Let me hold your face in my hands .
Let me look at you one last time .
Knowing that this is my end,
knowing you're all my heart yearn for .

All that shattered my soul
to be told "that's just how it is ".
Tell me I'm where I am supposed to be,
What I'm supposed to be ,
Tell me I was loved and cherished ,
Even if it's all a lie .
A mere act of sympathy ,
a wee bit of kindness , is all I ask.

Hold me close when My heart lies still ,
Leave my skin under the magnolia tree-
with your smell all over my soul .
Thread me through your ribs
and forget that I once loved you .
As you walk away from me,
Remember me as a stranger you never got to know.

I'll blend into your shadow ,
keep your feet warm at nights ,

I'll make sure your pillows are warm ,
And your showers cold as you like it .
I'll watch over the milk that's about to spill,
keep the roses in your vase, fresh .
Keep up with you in your walks -
Into what end there is for me.
My one last journey ,
To the journey of after-life .

2. A tiny little Rat

I am a tiny little rat
Trapped in a tiny little cage
I know how to free myself,
I know the trick
But why should I dig my grave .
Do i free myself from this tiny cage ,
Scraping my claws against the cold bar,
Go outside and pretend like I'm someone else ?
Or should I die right here ,
Chocking in my own solitude
Either way it's death ,
Either way it's painful ...

3. The mastermind of Mediocrity

The spring came with no hope whatsoever
Challenging the excruciating emotions inside you
You stood besides the window smoking
With an unbearable sigh of your mysery
Swooping your fingers across your ash dusted fringe
You held back the consciousness , the consequences
Of what filthy things you have undone
You lacked inspiration , a sense of your own self
With cruelty you wander around
The blood of innocent maidens in your hands
a dream soaked desire you embraced with no shame
Carried by the poisonous edge of your virility
The nights devoured your sleep ,Unable to breathe
Compunction tasted like graveyard dirt
Filling your insides with an ache you couldn't approach
You lost your heart to frostbite
But somehow the edges seem still alive
Warmth creeping through the cracks of your rib
Ignorance is a bliss isn't it
The imitations of a pretender ,
The falsity you wallow in .

You built a cathedral from your cruelty ,
In the altar you worshipped your own villainy
Who decides your fate Could it be me
Or the one who laid naked in a stable hay
A deliberately impotent man
How disappointing it must be ,
To be less than mediocrity
How disgraceful it is to be inferior than nothing
To be meagre , to be tiny , to be weaker than something.

4. The writer ; a paradox

I donot know how to unfold this feeling ,
this uncomfortable unsettling sensation ,
a rush of guilt , a bitterness
a mount of aspiration ;
The rush of rage and suffering at once
a feeling of self-loathing ; a bit of empathy
a feeling I'm indulging myself
in the trenches of agony .
I fell into the deep hole of sorrow
once in a while a hand pulled me up
and i laughed at the irony of my life
only to slip into the trenches again
only to be left alone with own thoughts .

They burned and carved words into my flesh .
They stared as I bled out to death .
Once in a while they put me to bed ,
only to wake up to the pain of my wounded heart.
This burning sensation upon my skin ,
am I aware of my own turns of fate ?
Feral is my teeth and nails turned out to be ,
yet you are the only one that I see.

Your tides and predicament that I feel ,
Am I you or are we one ?
Did I create you so I could be you?
Or did I create you to escape my own fate ?

Is this how a writer must feel,
to be devoured by their own imaginations .
To walk lengths into the oblivion ,
until your reflections fade .
To be the sacrifice it takes , to be heard .
I've walked miles from where i was ,
I ran and crawled and fell
and was carried by my own sins,
only to see you from a distance ;
To get a glance of your sweet innocence .
"Who are you and why do you exist ",
nobody answered my silent questions .
Yet I stayed and stared into your soul
Until i was a nothing but a puff of smoke .

An incommunicable feeling ,
an inexplicable explanation ,
a feeling in my bones ,
a hypersensitive concern ,
strangely abnormal confusion .

Am I sorrow or am I joy?
Am I nothing but a devastating piece of ruin ,
left between grief and love .
A dark tormented furor of passion ,
a deplorable mania to doubt my own existence .

No hunger no thirst ,
no urge to return to the normality of things .
I am full of perplexity and curves,
questions without answers ,
Screaming without an echo .
Am I intoxicated , did I lose my mind
or am I tipsy of how ironic it could be .
The mysery of the pawns i created ,
haunting me like a blood thirsty hound.

Am I slipping into something darker ?
Something outrageous as my soul .
An extravagant event I didn't propose .
A scandalous existence as if -
I'm slipping into the meaningful insanity
Or am I a writer ;
a senseless creature ;
Trying to make sense of the world ?
To understand

To be understood
To listen , to be heard
To love and to be loved .

5. A survivor's guilt.

I woke up in a hospital bed
Surrounded by the ghosts of my past
There was enough light to see
the depth of the terrible things I've done
People in white gowns looked at me with anger
A terrifying disgust , aching for a stranger
Like an alien i lied there with my eyes closed
comforted by the blue plastic blanket
wrapped around me like I'm a carcass
I couldn't stop but reminisce
The lake that i drowned in .

"What was the motive ?
What was the root cause?
Was this my impulsive stubbornness?
Or Was it to end it all ? "
A pinch of sympathy left behind
the lakes they drowned me in
A desparate grasp i ached for
a cry for help ; a final goodbye
the ones who found comfort
In watching their boots on my neck

Smiled with their crooked teeth
Staring into my lifeless body
Reaching out for a breathe
A moment of stillness, I craved
Was it ever so satisfying
to keep me inside the glass doors
To lock me in and feed me grapes
Was it ever so comforting to you soul?
to watch a child grow into madness,
An insanity you could never treat ?

I woke up in a hospital bed;
The day after you try to end your life
everything seems the same
even the cruelty in their eyes
A man who once called me his kin;
Never looked back at me again
But was there any love in him before
when I was invisible to his eyes
The day after you come back from death
People look at you with awe
They throw the baggage of sympathy they carry
only to be hit in the face by that
They fear you for having the guts
disgust you for the outrageous act
They show you their vocabulary

The meditations and therapies
A pool of pills and a recommendation or two
"Just read a book" they say
To not fall in love
To move on with your life
To be the one they wanted to see
They tell you find peace in living
and tell each other what a piece of shit you must be
to hurt the ones you love.

How would they know?
the years of battles you fought with yourself
How would they know
the days you felt helpless
The night you spend writing your own last goodbye
How will you show them your burned out insides
The scars you carved into yourself
The days you hid in the bathroom
scared of your own blood
How would you show them your insides
ripped open by the world outside
How could they ever understand
When they stood besides the ones who hurt you
They judge you , misinterpret you
They starve you for affection
For love ; for kindness

In the end, they walk away and
expect you to pick up your pieces and dance again
Call you a pretender , an impersonator
but all you were was a child
A child longing for affection
yearning for some kindness
A child born in pain
A child born out of nothingness.

In the end i as I laid there in a blue gown
The sweet memories i cuddled with
The terrifying aftermath
The pain in your mother's eyes
The fear in your father face
The little sister crying out of confusion
for all she knows she lost her kin
The one she loved , the one she kissed goodnight
Moments of your birth ,
passing like a movie scene in your mother's eyes
The first time you grabbed his fingers
your father as terrified as he is
The moment of realisation
The fear of lose
The mixed emotions outside the room
Was it ever worth it ?
Was it all a dream ?

Nobody answered as I know I don't deserve

The fear of exposed emotions
As exposed as I am ,
My wounds bled black
My worlds collide
In the end i realised
there was no ulterior motive
than to end my suffering and be long gone
To not carry my burned out wick until the end
To not carry my lifeless body through life
until I can rest it in my grave
But in between there was hope
There was guilt and pride
There was pain knowing i would never love again
That I would never kiss my sister goodnight
That i might not watch her grow up
That i might not share a meal with my own

In the end as burned out as I am
Trying again to ignite my flame
As it's easy to end it all
But to live the next day is what one must do
All the pain that I carry, I must rest
I must go on to the next day

Even though it might be ambivalent
I realised i burned out too soon
That the flame in me should be fueled again
I closed my eyes and tried to sleep
In the blue gown and plastic bed
To wake up the next day to hope
As they say everyday
This too shall pass ;
This too , shall pass...

6. Confessions of a believer.

I walked into the abyss
Reaching my hands out to the sky
Swallowing the sacred , drinking the water
Only to find god, to ask my question.

I walked into temples , chanting the mantras
Offering flowers , coconuts and garlands
A silent prayer to see you once
I didn't find a god nor peace or power .

I walked into a church Lighting the candles
joined the choir ,drank his blood; as prescribed
I prayed on my knees and worshipped the cross
I didn't find god , nor peace or power.

I walked into a wat , eyes closed all the way
Joined the charity ,I wore the clothes as said
falling asleep trying to meditate
I didn't find god nor peace or power.

I walked into a mosque; They said I cannot enter
As I am no man , As I am undeserving
I walked away knowing he might not be there

As what God wants a woman not to pray
She creates life like he intended
and I find no god , not even close anywhere.

The synagogue and shrines
All the places they worship him
I walked in and out , Knowing he isn't there
In the end I got tired of running
I went through my life knowing everything but him.

As I lay in my bed seeking death , despair
To see god in heaven, I prayed
A chill down my spine as terror spread its wings
the death stared into my soul and whispered
He does not exist .
he does not exist ?
He does not exist !

7. Don't look for me in my grave.

Don't look for me in my grave ,
Looking up to the sky to a star
Don't preach kindness in front of them
Gaining sympathy and condolence.

You think I was clueless as you dug my grave
Long before I died , your villainous plan
The terror behind my eyes As you tear the mask
An unheard cry I became , how tragic.

The floorboard creek with my weight
Even with no foot touching the ground
A fingerprint in your misty windows
The whisper behind your ears , no shadow .

As patient as rot , I wait
I drag my nails across the folds of your brain
To unfold your sleep with one eye closed

An unforgotten memory I became .

I teach the wallpaper to tear it's way down
Only to find blood , scattered;
You look for your friend , a barking irritation
Nowhere to be found as she sleeps forever

The air twitches in my shape , you blink
A quiet fear crawled it's way into your hair
A tilted frame , you blame stress
The chair swinging back and forth in stillness.

As you wake up into the terror you hide
To find dirt under your finger nails ,
The apologies you threw to empty rooms
Looking behind the curtains , just to be sure .

You shed a tear when you see my picture
With no guilt or grief, only a smile
The reflection blinked before you in the mirror
An abnormal breathe touched you in the shower .

I sleep rotting under your bed at nightfall
Expecting for your feet to touch the floor
A soft bruise at the back of your day
A door creek in distance ,
Your invitation, you dismiss in dread.

The keys misplaced , a song turned minor
A feeling of being watched , the uneasy terror
A quiet symphony uninvited ,
The keyholes you look through ,
A dramatic fall through the stairs.

The priests you seek , doctors and remedies
Answers you won't see in books and strangers
Endless prayers , the holy cross in your bed ;
the terror , the panick, a moment of realisation.

In the end as I drag you through the mud
A cry stuck in your throat , a painful melody
I'll dug you one next to me , in delight
As you bleed through the sand of my melancholy

You lie next to my grave
I leave some posies for your sake
Vengeance taste like dirt and iron
I'll walk into the light and disappear
the silence stays in your soul forever
As this is my win, my own glorious win .

8. The almost child.

I am the almost child
The almost of all things
Never quite there ;
never in between .

I am almost kind
Almost cruel as well
I am almost a poet ;
almost a stupid one .

I am almost empty
But almost filled
I am almost loved ;
But hated as well.

I am almost in love
It's almost a complexity
I am almost pretty ;
And almost unattractive .

I am almost right
And almost as wrong as you
I am almost the sun ;

But almost part of the moon.

I am almost a grown woman
But almost childish as well
I am almost a garden ;
But almost small as a flower .

I am almost enough
Never quite there
Never in between.
I am the almost child
And almost of all things.

9. The cotton flowers .

He thought that
I'll be frightened;
That I'll be scared of his sins
The carcass left in his cupboard
With skin and bones and wings.
He thought he could
Clasp it shut
And it will elude me
That I'll never see.
Little did he know
I was threading cotton flowers ;
Red and green And leaves
Into his carcass ;
weaving a garden into his sins.

10. My wounds ; Your blood.

The ruins of my love ,
A monument once i built with love;
Now stands alone
As the rain splatters across my face ,
Your image repulsively took over my memory
Inhaling as much as I can , i reminisced your face.
My memory as scattered as it is ,
Filled with your laughter , tea bags
And a book you left on my table .
I opened a page night after night
Only to feel your fingertips again .

A quiet cry you left behind my ears
Moaned as I thought about your face.
Moment stretched long since I embraced you smell ; Oh
your smell;
The burned ciggarettes and a vanilla cake
And the smell of an old book you kept in your study
The thin curves of your grin
The roughness of your chin ,your bare existence.
pale strands across your beard

"My snowman" I breathed
"My moonflower " you whispered.

I swallowed my pain dry
Oh the ache that left behind.
The anguish spread across my galaxies,
My morning coffee and my cigarette breaks .
I murmured your name every so often
Just to know if it's real , just to be sure .

You do see me
With Your sly half broken grin,
I see you too
Between the carved lines of time on your temples .
Somewhere a young man,
A handsome young man yearning to be held
Longing for my hands to reach his heart.
Your pulse echoed into my soul
Mine left in the emptyness of your absence .

Where was I wrong ?
Was i overreaching without ambition ?
Was it in the reaching ? Or the wanting ?
Was i so outrageously ignorant

To the nature of things,
Or was i just a girl , in love ?

The ruins of my love for you , it bleeds
It bleeds pink ,
I am what I am
The ruins of the monument I built once
Now stands alone
Once whole, now shattered by the moon
I was a corpse under the sun
As exposed as I am ;
my skin burned in mysery
My wounds deep , an echo of my soul
Nothing exists anymore .

I must walk away , I must
My footprints lost it's way back to yours.
The book once touched ,
Now swathed by a ghostly lace of longing.
An ear splitting scream struck to my throat
The silent oceans I cried
Now a crumbling parchment of my identity.

Love ; longing ; grief ,
to have known you, loved you ,
And to have lost you , i exist.
I see you now
But I must walk away ,
wearing the ruins like a grief woven veil
And i wear grief like a fucking veil.

11. When I'm older...

When I am older ,
I want a house with huge windows
A small house with my fingerprints colored
A long varandah that wraps around my entire home
plants that flower in spring
white curtains with laces stitched
With threads hanging out like it's undone
A glass window that opens to something green
I'll look out at the view-
While i sip my tea .
Some wooden sling chairs
the dead ones compared
A bedroom dark and cold ,
Memories hanging on the walls ,
I want a house with wooden floors
 blue tiles in the kitchen , the color of corals
a beautiful little backyard with every color of rose
A kitchen with light from each sides
A cookie jar in my dining table ,
to treat myself to something sweet
A long tall plant and yellow curtains all over
My blankets heavy and warm ,

So when I sleep alone,
I won't miss the warmth of a man
I want a rusty old radio ,
That stop when it moves
I'll sip my tea and watch the rainy weather
Cold sweet snow and summers pass
And as autumn came by with its melancholic music,
I would cry and cry for everything I've lost
I'd live my life as I'm the only one
born and died alone
and as I sip my tea into my old age
I'd sing for the men that passed this way
I'd sing for the ones who died in my arms
And the ones who died running away...

12. Maternal blues

How does it feel to lose everything ,
Everything all at once ?
To lose love , to lose hope
To lose yourself , and the only one you love .

How does it feel to forget your existence
To concede in my fate ;
To float towards an ending ,unknown.

How does it feel to witness-
the sand seeping through your fingers
To know you can't help but watch.

Like a dandelion in the wind-
I watched you drift away ,
as i stood there mesmerized,
A child stargazing , nothing but a surprise.

When my warm yellow sheets bloomed red
Your existence as mellow it was ,
oozed out of the home I made for you
and you made me wonder if I wasnt good enough,
to hold you in my arms.
To call you my baby , oh sweet child
I wonder if I wasn't good enough.

I didn't move an inch ; neither did i cry
I twisted my tangled hair with my fingers
As the slow ache reached my throat
My cries dissolved inside as I swallowed the pain.
Only to lay there still,
only to pretend you linger still.

Did it hurt, to be parted from me ?
Was it painful to leave home,
to be exposed into a world you weren't ready for ?
Did you cry for me , one last cry ?
Did you hope that I will hold you
to help you out of your distress ?
I wonder if you knew that I'm real
The lullabies I sang, did you ever listen ?
Did you know me at all?
Did you feel it when I giggled ?

Did you know that i cried ?

My heart aches knowing you are gone.
My life crumbled into a single "why"
What am I from now on ?
What was I before you - I can't remember
Was I ever complete, happy or sad?
what did I crave ? What did i resent ?
My heart set to Mozart , a dramatic cry
Falling down the stairs of confusion
All the "why"s I cannot comprehend
Yet I lay here , a nobody .

Did I ever have you?
The nights I pretend to sing for you,
the nights I spend reading to you.
Did you feel my warmth?
when you kicked me
Were you mad that I was still awake?

What was i after you ?
I am no mother as I don't have you
I carried you and yet

I donot have you in my arms
I cannot feed you -
yet my bosom leaks to the thought of you
I am no mother -
Yet I still bleed in my bed
Who am I without you , my child
Am I still a mother ? My daughter
Without you who am I
I am no mother and yet-
I grieve for the baby i never had ...

13. The final chase.

I ran as fast as I could
to hide my skin , exposed
Through the mud and mountains ,
through the knee deep waters .

I was ten; I ran for my life
Naked and scared, a vulnerable prey
Running through a forest full of seekers .
Predators and hunters they were ,
looking for vulnerability,
looking for children.

The feral souls watched me
as I sprinted through the forest .
a white cat followed me into the river
Only to corner and watch me fall.

I was caught in a moment ,
how predictable I must be .
They chained me to the tree
With a long golden chain
They claimed I should be free
the shallow hopes it brought it me,

Oh how tragic it all must be .

They peeled me off ,layer by layer
to see if I'm fairer inside ;
to see if I'm worthy ; to see if I'm pure,
only to savor my skin and bones.
My pliant flesh swirled in dirt
thrown off to the wild ones who hizzed
A barefoot naked child , helpless as I am
stood quiet , embracing my end
a whisper instead of a scream ,
a breathe instead of a cry , I remained still
Yet ,Death was unkind .

They cut off my ears ;Crawled out my eyes
a bone deep void at rest
They preyed on the darkness ,
They eat out my carcass ,
Until I was nothing but a frame draped in flesh.

Their hunger carved me to the bone,
I thrashed , but silence held me still.
My heart crawls slow, a rusted drum
I am alive enough to feel I am dead.

14. The girl in the passenger seat.

Little girl in the passenger seat
Smile as wide as her face
Glimmering eyes and a heart untouched by the world
Holding her doll , a little doll in pink skirt
Watching out the city lights ,
Frozen in awe.

Little girl in the passenger seat ,
In familiarity, she was safe
Families matter -
Even the monsters deserve a smile.
She held onto her pretty doll-
a moment of disbelief - fear
a childish gester shifting-
a horrifying moment of consternation.

Little girl in the passenger seat
Unable to understand the cruelty
the monster ripped her innocence apart
even in daze, a smile lingered her lips
The road twisted on without pause
a day turned an eternity

her childhood disappeared;
All she saw was fear -
in the crowd ,the monsters smiled
Shadows in the alley
Time went on; she still smiled .

Little girl in the passenger sear
With age she became smaller
Her head wrapped around her eyes
as blind she kept on walking
the monsters in the crowd in dreams
Taking over her sleep, her home
she grabbed onto her doll in pink
watching the world pass by her side

Little girl in the passenger seat ;
There she sat, steadfast, as the hours drifted past
looking for the monster who stole her childhood
looking through crowds for him
with courage, to take it back.
Someday she will find her childhood again ,
Someday she will smile ;
Until then she'll grab onto the doll in pink
Waiting for the girl in passenger seat...

15. In the hour of parting.

No flower compares -
not the endless sky above
not the soulful blue sea
outshines my woman's love

Into the fathoms of her brown eyes , I fall
Where an eternal light kept chaste- her smile
as tender as her pout - her kiss
for her, I'll greet the end in thaw

Toward the mountain's height , i walk
with darkness weighing my shadow
her longing shows the light above
a bashful glance , a flicker light
She greets me where I drop my pride

Her veils-tailing , kissing the hearth
a spellbinding melody , yet unnamed
not the hearth that kindle the chamber, but she
a whisper around the doorway
a gaze , timid yet tender
I near , she nods in grace
my sweet woman your love

Her long curly hair that tangle in the wind ,
she tames it with a wooden comb
I sit watching her in awe
She blush and gaze out the window
Her smile, with that tiny fleck on snout
she giggles and whispers and cries when it rains
her smile greets the butterflies fluttering near

She is love made flesh and I ,
a fortunate soul beholds it each dawn
The luckiest of men, I am
to be hers and hers alone
And this battle might take my body in pieces
But her love will carry me home , each dawn
eternal and unbroken ,
My woman's love will carry me home...

16. I remain.

I fear I fall in love anew,
with the cold hands that gently stray,
I dare not kiss your wounds and cry
As you are death and I am alive
I breathe to glimpse your face someday
To belong to you - if only for a day
The beauty you are, I dream of still,
a painless sleep to bear my will .

I yearn for you - a final breathe
To undo the days gone by and the hours ahead
to carry my guilt and my regret ,
Lend me your hands and forgive my sins ;
Forgive the unforgivable deeds I did
My sins float in the river as I lay
like a cichlid floating with its child.

I pass my days in quiet plea,
that you might come uncalled for me.
touch your cold hands above my soul
take me away from this mascarade called life.

If only you would open your arms for me
I shall collapse into your ribs rotting in mud
I shall forget the life's bitter farce
And see the light beyond the rainbow
I shall lay still and let the earth swallow me whole
the flowers might take over my skin and bones
Blooming black roses from ashes of my bones.

While i twist and turn in my grave
I dream your pale grip clasp on me
I will melt into your darkness -
swim around in your oceans and
rest the ache i carry in me , once and for all
I will whimper and wale and weep into your chill
and when my tears run dry - I will rest forever.

Call me into the fate you keep for me ;
I am weary enough to rest my sorrow.
Smother me with kindness - an end.
let me breathe through my pain , just once
This loneliness consumes me still
seek me when I sleep-
Carry me to my grave in your arms

my tears will wait till then,
Go, for i remain...

17. The day after you.

The bed is cold
I lay where you used to
Your favourite pillow ,
Now lying still ; like it knows
That you're not coming back.
The emptyness I inhale
It tastes sour as my tears
Somehow it bites my back
And I am nothing but an ache
Lingering onto the room
Yearning for a call from the other room .

The coffee cup you left in the sink
It stains the counter like a bruise
Your brush leaned on mine
Your towel smells of your sweat
My hands burned when I touched your clothes
I opened the curtains ;
It's too bright for my eyes
Your smell still lingers in the closet
I hoped your jacket to move
To embrace me and cry with me
And tell me it will be fine

The sound of your shoes coming in
I stared into the way
My brain plays tricks like
I saw you walking away
My wet hair is dripping out to the sheets
If you were here then
You would dry it with a sheet
You would play with my hair ,
And joke about something lame
And i would laugh to your innocence
As I say " that's so sweet "

I inhaled your smell that's
Lingering on our sheets
It's not enough
Not at all
Yet I swallowed it whole
I scream your name
Hoping you would run to me
Nobody replied
Only silence stayed
It pressed me against the walls
Into the sheets
Until I could hear my heartbeat on my head

The sun moves across the floorboard
Yet it's ignoring me
I eat because I'm told
But everything tastes like dirt
I can't remember the last time
You called my name or how .

My memories are fading and
I can't remember the last thing you said
I am beginning to fall into the void
Or this empty house of a world
The way my fingers fit in yours,
I am starting to forget when .
Time is erasing you like it's written in sand
And my grief can't catch up to the speed

I am alone
The silence is eating me alive
I swallow my pain and
Hope I won't wake up from my sleep
My heart keeps beating ,
Unreasonable it seems
Yet I hear an echo ,
As " you are nothing but waiting "....

18. To my father; with Love.

I was there ,
Sitting still
Clawing my fingertips-
Into my palms,
Counting the seconds between their laughter
Watching his forced smile
In his eyes ,
he was shrinking ,
hoping they would stop.

They laughed at him-
not loud .
Loud enough for me to hear
and for him to pretend he didn't.
He stood there with a fake smile ,
He said nothing -
Yet his eyes ,wet ;
I know he was crying a river inside .

They laughed at his job ,
his worn shirt

and his grey hair
They asked questions he couldn't answer
They made him their prey-
Disguised as a "joke"
and I , a helpless daughter .

They called him by his name ,
even though they were younger .
He didn't have any money - they said
Might as well as shrink him,
to the earth- they thought.

I wanted to cut them with my words
but a child taught to be polite ,
couldn't raise her voice
Against the cruelty of elders.
I spend my life rehearsing ,
The strike of words i held inside.

They saw his calluses and
a quiet tone ,
and they thought it all meant less;
but little did they know that
those hands built our home ,

Everything we have ,
And more.

They walked it off-
as if it was a joke,
as if it didn't shape a reflection -
a cruel reflection
he saw in himself,
and little do they know he still carry it.
He carries it to this day,
the shame,
the insecurity ,
and the forced smile.

My father -
His heart knows no guile,
And his kin-
Vultures preying on the innocent.
They tore him apart,
in the name of a joke ,
and yet he smiles at them-
like an innocent child ,
in the middle of chaos.

19. A funeral for our adulthood.

People say they lost their childhood
Between their mother's rage-
Between their father's cold stares.
Yet nobody knows-
No-one about the adulthood they lost
performing for survival.
"I'm fine" they lie
to be seen normal,
to fit in.
They stand at the funeral of their adulthood
without even knowing
that the years they lost
Trying to know themselves,
Trying not to be blue,
to be somebody.
They don't see their soul-
burned out,
Reaching for the love beyond,
just to feel the warmth of someone.
licking the sweetness off their knives ,
to feel better ,
to be heard , loved-

to be seen.
They bring flowers to their own grave
never shed a tear , yet
Carry the guilt-the shame,
the abandonment ;
They carry it in their head,
their chest , in their words,
to the next relationship; a friendship.
They try hard not to show
through the cracks-
of the smile they drew on their faces,
between the sunken eyes .
They pass it on to the ones around
shape their reality,
their personality,
thinking "that's just me " ;
When all it is,
the ashes from their own grave,
of their adulthood.
The adult who died ,
Choking in the dirt of their childhood.

20. Hope is a big fat dog.

And when I woke up,
the life I knew was gone.
The sunlight didn't sting anymore
It dragged it's veil through the wooden floor-
leaving a warm hug in the bed.

My eyes and lips still wear their bruise
But the pain is softer than yesterday.
My throat is dry and face is pale
But I can feel a new life blooming again.

My baby still asleep,
in the home I made her-
beneath my ribs ,
beneath my skin .
As warm and safe as she is ,
I feel her sweet hands reaching
for the new life rooting in my soul.

I walked past the rooms ,
The ones still haunted by my cries,
The one I was left to starve in
And the one I almost died in .

A quiet cry followed me to the kitchen,
the one that smells of stale afternoons.
I picked the cold bread crumbs ,
and ate them like a stranger to food.

My white dress was stained red ,
but yet i felt so yellow .
My baby twirled with each bite ,
my hair felt like freedom.

I opened the door and met the world-
the breeze was cold, but it felt alive.
I walked into the untamed woods-
Where the red flowers refused to hide.
I turned my eyes once again,
Towards the kitchen floor,
My kitchen floor ;
To see my husband, 'The apple of my eye'-
face down on the wooden floor ,
stabbed by the life he thought he owned.

He looked handsome as ever ,
with his face drained of blood
And his chest with my knife inside,
finally quiet, his face no longer scary.
And for the first time in years ,
I smiled with my whole heart .

Hope is a big fat dog ,
chasing me through the woods tonight.
I might die here tomorrow,
Yet it's barks will keep me alive.

21. As the final act of Love ;

And as the final act of love,
I will give myself everything
I'll climb my way out of the trenches
of deep dead conversations-
rotting as time goes on;
and I will leave it there to decompose ;
To be a mere memory.
And I won't touch it until it's nothing but dust,
only to blow it into the wind .

And as the final act of love ,
I'll sweep the noise out my head .
I will polish the edges of my brain ,
And let it catch the light as long as it can.
I would silence my thoughts,
so they may shine forever ;
In the empty chambers of my skull.

And as the final act of love ,
I will let go of all that exists ;
knowing I'll never be able to hold it again.

Watching them drift away - will be the moment ,
I will see how momentary they were .
How hopeless it is to love , to trust and to care .

And as the final act of love ,
I would scrub the floors of my memory ,
I will keep every item I find in the corners,hiding .
I will relive the moments I once loved ,
the ones I cried about , the ones I lost and won.

And as the final act of love ,
I will hug myself ;
"It's alright " I'll say,
And I'll bring solace to my soul
I'll unburden myself of all , not just hate
The guilt. The Love . The Terror .The Desire.

And as the final act of love ,
I'll embrace my tormented desire-
I will disappear ;
I will light a ciggarette and watch it burn slow
And when it's gone , so will I.

As the final act of self love ,
I'll forgive my sins and forget my name
I'll be a nobody ; but I will be free...